MW00947551

Welcome

To: _____

At: _____

Wifi Code: _____

Our telephone number:

_____

Enjoy Your Stay

We love guest feedback..

It helps us make your stay as
special as we possibly can...

A guest book is a story told by
many people, so please share
your memories, favorite activities,
places to eat and things to see.

Rest Relax Recharge

Guest name(s) ....

Arrived .... Departed ....

Where did you travel from? ....

Best Places to Eat/Drink: ....

....

Places to Visit/Attractions: ....

....

Favorite Memories: ....

....

....

Message to Host: ....

....

....

Guest name(s) ....

Arrived .... Departed ....

Where did you travel from ? ....

Best Places to Eat/Drink : ....

....

Places to Visit/Attractions : ....

....

Favorite Memories: ....

....

....

Message to Host: ....

....

....

Guest name(s) ....

Arrived .... Departed ....

Where did you travel from? ....

Best Places to Eat/Drink :...

....

Places to Visit/Attractions : ....

....

Favorite Memories: ....

....

....

Message to Host: ....

....

....

Guest name(s) ....

Arrived .... Departed ....

Where did you travel from ? ....

Best Places to Eat/Drink : ....

....

Places to Visit/Attractions : ....

....

Favorite Memories: ....

....

....

Message to Host: ....

....

....

Guest name(s) ....

Arrived .... Departed ....

Where did you travel from? ....

Best Places to Eat/Drink : ....

....

Places to Visit/Attractions : ....

....

Favorite Memories: ....

....

....

Message to Host: ....

....

....

Guest name(s) ....

Arrived .... Departed ....

Where did you travel from? ....

Best Places to Eat/Drink: ....

....

Places to Visit/Attractions: ....

....

Favorite Memories: ....

....

....

Message to Host: ....

....

....

Guest name(s) ....

Arrived .... Departed ....

Where did you travel from? ....

Best Places to Eat/Drink : ....

....

Places to Visit/Attractions : ....

....

Favorite Memories: ....

....

....

Message to Host: ....

....

....

Guest name(s) ....

Arrived .... Departed ....

Where did you travel from? ....

Best Places to Eat/Drink : ....

....

Places to Visit/Attractions : ....

....

Favorite Memories: ....

....

....

Message to Host: ....

....

....

Guest name(s) ....

Arrived .... Departed ....

Where did you travel from? ....

Best Places to Eat/Drink : ....

....

Places to Visit/Attractions : ....

....

Favorite Memories: ....

....

....

Message to Host: ....

....

....

Guest name(s) ....

Arrived .... Departed ....

Where did you travel from ? ....

Best Places to Eat / Drink : ....

....

Places to Visit / Attractions : ....

....

Favorite Memories: ....

....

....

Message to Host: ....

....

....

Guest name(s) ....

Arrived .... Departed ....

Where did you travel from? ....

Best Places to Eat/Drink : ....

....

Places to Visit/Attractions : ....

....

Favorite Memories: ....

....

....

Message to Host: ....

....

....

Guest name(s) ....

Arrived .... Departed ....

Where did you travel from ? ....

Best Places to Eat/Drink : ....

....

Places to Visit/Attractions : ....

....

Favorite Memories: ....

....

....

Message to Host: ....

....

....

Guest name(s) ....

Arrived .... Departed ....

Where did you travel from? ....

Best Places to Eat/Drink : ....

....

Places to Visit/Attractions : ....

....

Favorite Memories: ....

....

....

Message to Host: ....

....

....

Guest name(s) ....

Arrived .... Departed ....

Where did you travel from? ....

Best Places to Eat/Drink: ....

....

Places to Visit/Attractions: ....

....

Favorite Memories: ....

....

....

Message to Host: ....

....

....

Guest name(s) ....

Arrived .... Departed ....

Where did you travel from? ....

Best Places to Eat/Drink : ....

....

Places to Visit/Attractions : ....

....

Favorite Memories: ....

....

....

Message to Host: ....

....

....

Guest name(s) ....

Arrived .... Departed ....

Where did you travel from? ....

Best Places to Eat/Drink: ....

....

Places to Visit/Attractions: ....

....

Favorite Memories: ....

....

....

Message to Host: ....

....

....

Guest name(s) ....

Arrived .... Departed ....

Where did you travel from? ....

Best Places to Eat/Drink: ....

....

Places to Visit/Attractions: ....

....

Favorite Memories: ....

....

....

Message to Host: ....

....

....

Guest name(s) ....

Arrived .... Departed ....

Where did you travel from ? ....

Best Places to Eat/Drink : ....

....

Places to Visit/Attractions : ....

....

Favorite Memories: ....

....

....

Message to Host: ....

....

....

Guest name(s) ....

Arrived .... Departed ....

Where did you travel from? ....

Best Places to Eat/Drink: ....

....

Places to Visit/Attractions: ....

....

Favorite Memories: ....

....

....

Message to Host: ....

....

....

Guest name(s) ....

Arrived .... Departed ....

Where did you travel from? ....

Best Places to Eat/Drink: ....

....

Places to Visit/Attractions: ....

....

Favorite Memories: ....

....

....

Message to Host: ....

....

....

Guest name(s) ....

Arrived .... Departed ....

Where did you travel from? ....

Best Places to Eat/Drink: ....

....

Places to Visit/Attractions: ....

....

Favorite Memories: ....

....

....

Message to Host: ....

....

....

Guest name(s) ....

Arrived .... Departed ....

Where did you travel from? ....

Best Places to Eat/Drink : ....

....

Places to Visit/Attractions : ....

....

Favorite Memories: ....

....

....

Message to Host: ....

....

....

Guest name(s) ....

Arrived .... Departed ....

Where did you travel from ? ....

Best Places to Eat/Drink : ....

....

Places to Visit/Attractions : ....

....

Favorite Memories: ....

....

....

Message to Host: ....

....

....

Guest name(s) ....

Arrived .... Departed ....

Where did you travel from? ....

Best Places to Eat/Drink: ....

....

Places to Visit/Attractions: ....

....

Favorite Memories: ....

....

....

Message to Host: ....

....

....

Guest name(s) ....

Arrived .... Departed ....

Where did you travel from? ....

Best Places to Eat/Drink :..

....

Places to Visit/Attractions : ....

....

Favorite Memories: ....

....

....

Message to Host: ....

....

....

Guest name(s) ....

Arrived .... Departed ....

Where did you travel from ? ....

Best Places to Eat / Drink : ....

....

Places to Visit / Attractions : ....

....

Favorite Memories: ....

....

....

Message to Host: ....

....

....

Guest name(s) ....

Arrived .... Departed ....

Where did you travel from ? ....

Best Places to Eat / Drink : ....

....

Places to Visit / Attractions : ....

....

Favorite Memories: ....

....

....

Message to Host: ....

....

....

Guest name(s) ....

Arrived .... Departed ....

Where did you travel from? ....

Best Places to Eat/Drink: ....

....

Places to Visit/Attractions: ....

....

Favorite Memories: ....

....

....

Message to Host: ....

....

....

Guest name(s) ....

Arrived .... Departed ....

Where did you travel from? ....

Best Places to Eat/Drink : ....

....

Places to Visit/Attractions : ....

....

Favorite Memories: ....

....

....

Message to Host: ....

....

....

Guest name(s) ....

Arrived .... Departed ....

Where did you travel from ? ....

Best Places to Eat / Drink : ....

....

Places to Visit / Attractions : ....

....

Favorite Memories: ....

....

....

Message to Host: ....

....

....

Guest name(s) ....

Arrived .... Departed ....

Where did you travel from? ....

Best Places to Eat/Drink : ....

....

Places to Visit/Attractions : ....

....

Favorite Memories: ....

....

....

Message to Host: ....

....

....

Guest name(s) ....

Arrived .... Departed ....

Where did you travel from? ....

Best Places to Eat/Drink: ....

....

Places to Visit/Attractions: ....

....

Favorite Memories: ....

....

....

Message to Host: ....

....

....

Guest name(s) ....

Arrived .... Departed ....

Where did you travel from? ....

Best Places to Eat/Drink : ....

....

Places to Visit/Attractions : ....

....

Favorite Memories: ....

....

....

Message to Host: ....

....

....

Guest name(s) ....

Arrived .... Departed ....

Where did you travel from ? ....

Best Places to Eat/Drink : ....

....

Places to Visit/Attractions : ....

....

Favorite Memories: ....

....

....

Message to Host: ....

....

....

Guest name(s) ....

Arrived .... Departed ....

Where did you travel from? ....

Best Places to Eat/Drink : ....

....

Places to Visit/Attractions : ....

....

Favorite Memories: ....

....

....

Message to Host: ....

....

....

Guest name(s) ....

Arrived .... Departed ....

Where did you travel from ? ....

Best Places to Eat/Drink : ....

....

Places to Visit/Attractions : ....

....

Favorite Memories: ....

....

....

Message to Host: ....

....

....

Guest name(s) ....

Arrived .... Departed ....

Where did you travel from? ....

Best Places to Eat/Drink : ....

....

Places to Visit/Attractions : ....

....

Favorite Memories: ....

....

....

Message to Host: ....

....

....

Guest name(s) ....

Arrived .... Departed ....

Where did you travel from? ....

Best Places to Eat/Drink: ....

....

Places to Visit/Attractions: ....

....

Favorite Memories: ....

....

....

Message to Host: ....

....

....

Guest name(s) ....

Arrived .... Departed ....

Where did you travel from? ....

Best Places to Eat/Drink : ....

....

Places to Visit/Attractions : ....

....

Favorite Memories: ....

....

....

Message to Host: ....

....

....

Guest name(s) ....

Arrived .... Departed ....

Where did you travel from ? ....

Best Places to Eat/Drink : ....

....

Places to Visit/Attractions : ....

....

Favorite Memories: ....

....

....

Message to Host: ....

....

....

Guest name(s) ....

Arrived .... Departed ....

Where did you travel from ? ....

Best Places to Eat/Drink : ....

....

Places to Visit/Attractions : ....

....

Favorite Memories: ....

....

....

Message to Host: ....

....

....

Guest name(s) ....

Arrived .... Departed ....

Where did you travel from? ....

Best Places to Eat/Drink: ....

....

Places to Visit/Attractions: ....

....

Favorite Memories: ....

....

....

Message to Host: ....

....

....

Guest name(s) ....

Arrived .... Departed ....

Where did you travel from? ....

Best Places to Eat/Drink : ....

....

Places to Visit/Attractions : ....

....

Favorite Memories: ....

....

....

Message to Host: ....

....

....

Guest name(s) ....

Arrived .... Departed ....

Where did you travel from? ....

Best Places to Eat/Drink: ....

....

Places to Visit/Attractions: ....

....

Favorite Memories: ....

....

....

Message to Host: ....

....

....

Guest name(s) ....

Arrived .... Departed ....

Where did you travel from ? ....

Best Places to Eat/Drink :.....................................

....

Places to Visit/Attractions : ....

....

Favorite Memories: ....

....

....

Message to Host: ....

....

....

Guest name(s) ....

Arrived .... Departed ....

Where did you travel from? ....

Best Places to Eat/Drink: ....

....

Places to Visit/Attractions: ....

....

Favorite Memories: ....

....

....

Message to Host: ....

....

....

Guest name(s) ....

Arrived .... Departed ....

Where did you travel from ? ....

Best Places to Eat/Drink : ....

....

Places to Visit/Attractions : ....

....

Favorite Memories: ....

....

....

Message to Host: ....

....

....

Guest name(s) ....

Arrived .... Departed ....

Where did you travel from ? ....

Best Places to Eat/Drink : ....

....

Places to Visit/Attractions : ....

....

Favorite Memories: ....

....

....

Message to Host: ....

....

....

Guest name(s) ....

Arrived .... Departed ....

Where did you travel from? ....

Best Places to Eat/Drink : ....

....

Places to Visit/Attractions : ....

....

Favorite Memories: ....

....

....

Message to Host: ....

....

....

Guest name(s) ....

Arrived .... Departed ....

Where did you travel from? ....

Best Places to Eat/Drink: ....

....

Places to Visit/Attractions: ....

....

Favorite Memories: ....

....

....

Message to Host: ....

....

....

Guest name(s) ....

Arrived .... Departed ....

Where did you travel from ? ....

Best Places to Eat/Drink : ....

....

Places to Visit/Attractions : ....

....

Favorite Memories: ....

....

....

Message to Host: ....

....

....

Guest name(s) ....

Arrived .... Departed ....

Where did you travel from ? ....

Best Places to Eat/Drink : ....

....

Places to Visit/Attractions : ....

....

Favorite Memories: ....

....

....

Message to Host: ....

....

....

Guest name(s) ....

Arrived .... Departed ....

Where did you travel from? ....

Best Places to Eat/Drink: ....

....

Places to Visit/Attractions: ....

....

Favorite Memories: ....

....

....

Message to Host: ....

....

....

Guest name(s) ....

Arrived .... Departed ....

Where did you travel from ? ....

Best Places to Eat / Drink : ....

....

Places to Visit / Attractions : ....

....

Favorite Memories: ....

....

....

Message to Host: ....

....

....

Guest name(s) ....

Arrived .... Departed ....

Where did you travel from? ....

Best Places to Eat/Drink : ....
....

Places to Visit/Attractions : ....
....

Favorite Memories: ....
....

....

Message to Host: ....
....

....

Guest name(s) ....

Arrived .... Departed ....

Where did you travel from? ....

Best Places to Eat/Drink : ....

....

Places to Visit/Attractions : ....

....

Favorite Memories: ....

....

....

Message to Host: ....

....

....

Guest name(s) ....

Arrived .... Departed ....

Where did you travel from ? ....

Best Places to Eat/Drink : ....

....

Places to Visit/Attractions : ....

....

Favorite Memories: ....

....

....

Message to Host: ....

....

....

Guest name(s) ....

Arrived .... Departed ....

Where did you travel from ? ....

Best Places to Eat / Drink : ....

....

Places to Visit / Attractions : ....

....

Favorite Memories: ....

....

....

Message to Host: ....

....

....

Guest name(s) ....

Arrived .... Departed ....

Where did you travel from? ....

Best Places to Eat/Drink :.....................................

....

Places to Visit/Attractions : ....

....

Favorite Memories: ....

....

....

Message to Host: ....

....

....

Guest name(s) ....

Arrived .... Departed ....

Where did you travel from ? ....

Best Places to Eat/Drink : ....

....

Places to Visit/Attractions : ....

....

Favorite Memories: ....

....

....

Message to Host: ....

....

....

Guest name(s) ....

Arrived .... Departed ....

Where did you travel from? ....

Best Places to Eat/Drink: ....

....

Places to Visit/Attractions: ....

....

Favorite Memories: ....

....

....

Message to Host: ....

....

....

Guest name(s) ....

Arrived .... Departed ....

Where did you travel from ? ....

Best Places to Eat / Drink : ....

....

Places to Visit / Attractions : ....

....

Favorite Memories: ....

....

....

Message to Host: ....

....

....

Guest name(s) ....

Arrived .... Departed ....

Where did you travel from ? ....

Best Places to Eat/Drink : ....

....

Places to Visit/Attractions : ....

.

....

Favorite Memories: ....

....

....

Message to Host: ....

....

....

Guest name(s) ....

Arrived .... Departed ....

Where did you travel from ? ....

Best Places to Eat/Drink : ....

....

Places to Visit/Attractions : ....

....

Favorite Memories: ....

....

....

Message to Host: ....

....

....

Guest name(s) ....

Arrived .... Departed ....

Where did you travel from? ....

Best Places to Eat/Drink : ....

....

Places to Visit/Attractions : ....

....

Favorite Memories: ....

....

....

Message to Host: ....

....

....

Guest name(s) ....

Arrived .... Departed ....

Where did you travel from ? ....

Best Places to Eat/Drink : ....

....

Places to Visit/Attractions : ....

....

Favorite Memories: ....

....

....

Message to Host: ....

....

....

Guest name(s) ....

Arrived .... Departed ....

Where did you travel from? ....

Best Places to Eat/Drink : ....

....

Places to Visit/Attractions : ....

....

Favorite Memories: ....

....

....

Message to Host: ....

....

....

Guest name(s) ....

Arrived .... Departed ....

Where did you travel from ? ....

Best Places to Eat / Drink : ....

....

Places to Visit / Attractions : ....

....

Favorite Memories: ....

....

....

Message to Host: ....

....

....

Guest name(s) ....

Arrived .... Departed ....

Where did you travel from? ....

Best Places to Eat/Drink : ....

....

Places to Visit/Attractions : ....

....

Favorite Memories: ....

....

....

Message to Host: ....

....

....

Guest name(s) ....

Arrived .... Departed ....

Where did you travel from ? ....

Best Places to Eat / Drink : ....

....

Places to Visit / Attractions : ....

....

Favorite Memories: ....

....

....

Message to Host: ....

....

....

Guest name(s) ....

Arrived .... Departed ....

Where did you travel from? ....

Best Places to Eat/Drink : ....
....

Places to Visit/Attractions : ....
....

Favorite Memories: ....
....
....

Message to Host: ....
....
....

Guest name(s) ....

Arrived .... Departed ....

Where did you travel from? ....

Best Places to Eat/Drink: ....

....

Places to Visit/Attractions: ....

....

Favorite Memories: ....

....

....

Message to Host: ....

....

....

Guest name(s) ....

Arrived .... Departed ....

Where did you travel from? ....

Best Places to Eat/Drink :.......................................

....

Places to Visit/Attractions : ....

....

Favorite Memories: ....

....

....

Message to Host: ....

....

....

Guest name(s) ....

Arrived .... Departed ....

Where did you travel from ? ....

Best Places to Eat / Drink : ....

....

Places to Visit / Attractions : ....

....

Favorite Memories: ....

....

....

Message to Host: ....

....

....

Guest name(s) ....

Arrived .... Departed ....

Where did you travel from? ....

Best Places to Eat/Drink : ....

....

Places to Visit/Attractions : ....

....

Favorite Memories: ....

....

....

Message to Host: ....

....

....

Guest name(s) ....

Arrived .... Departed ....

Where did you travel from? ....

Best Places to Eat/Drink: ....

....

Places to Visit/Attractions: ....

....

Favorite Memories: ....

....

....

Message to Host: ....

....

....

Guest name(s) ....

Arrived .... Departed ....

Where did you travel from? ....

Best Places to Eat/Drink : ....

....

Places to Visit/Attractions : ....

....

Favorite Memories: ....

....

....

Message to Host: ....

....

....

Guest name(s) ....

Arrived .... Departed ....

Where did you travel from ? ....

Best Places to Eat/Drink : ....

....

Places to Visit/Attractions : ....

....

Favorite Memories: ....

....

....

Message to Host: ....

....

....

Guest name(s) ....

Arrived .... Departed ....

Where did you travel from ? ....

Best Places to Eat/Drink : ....

....

Places to Visit/Attractions : ....

....

Favorite Memories: ....

....

....

Message to Host: ....

....

....

Guest name(s) ....

Arrived .... Departed ....

Where did you travel from ? ....

Best Places to Eat/Drink : ....

....

Places to Visit/Attractions : ....

....

Favorite Memories: ....

....

....

Message to Host: ....

....

....

Guest name(s) ....

Arrived .... Departed ....

Where did you travel from? ....

Best Places to Eat/Drink : ....

....

Places to Visit/Attractions : ....

....

Favorite Memories: ....

....

....

Message to Host: ....

....

....

Guest name(s) ....

Arrived .... Departed ....

Where did you travel from ? ....

Best Places to Eat/Drink : ....

....

Places to Visit/Attractions : ....

....

Favorite Memories: ....

....

....

Message to Host: ....

....

....

Guest name(s) ....

Arrived .... Departed ....

Where did you travel from? ....

Best Places to Eat/Drink : ....

....

Places to Visit/Attractions : ....

....

Favorite Memories: ....

....

....

Message to Host: ....

....

....

Guest name(s) ....

Arrived .... Departed ....

Where did you travel from? ....

Best Places to Eat/Drink: ....

....

Places to Visit/Attractions: ....

....

Favorite Memories: ....

....

....

Message to Host: ....

....

....

Guest name(s) ....

Arrived .... Departed ....

Where did you travel from ? ....

Best Places to Eat/Drink : ....

....

Places to Visit/Attractions : ....

....

Favorite Memories: ....

....

....

Message to Host: ....

....

....

Guest name(s) ....

Arrived .... Departed ....

Where did you travel from ? ....

Best Places to Eat / Drink : ....

....

Places to Visit / Attractions : ....

....

Favorite Memories: ....

....

....

Message to Host: ....

....

....

Guest name(s) ....

Arrived .... Departed ....

Where did you travel from? ....

Best Places to Eat/Drink : ....

....

Places to Visit/Attractions : ....

....

Favorite Memories: ....

....

....

Message to Host: ....

....

....

Guest name(s) ....

Arrived .... Departed ....

Where did you travel from ? ....

Best Places to Eat / Drink : ....

....

Places to Visit / Attractions : ....

....

Favorite Memories: ....

....

....

Message to Host: ....

....

....

Guest name(s) ....

Arrived .... Departed ....

Where did you travel from? ....

Best Places to Eat/Drink : ....

....

Places to Visit/Attractions : ....

....

Favorite Memories: ....

....

....

Message to Host: ....

....

....

Guest name(s) ....

Arrived .... Departed ....

Where did you travel from ? ....

Best Places to Eat/Drink : ....

....

Places to Visit/Attractions : ....

....

Favorite Memories: ....

....

....

Message to Host: ....

....

....

Guest name(s) ....

Arrived .... Departed ....

Where did you travel from? ....

Best Places to Eat/Drink: ....

....

Places to Visit/Attractions: ....

....

Favorite Memories: ....

....

....

Message to Host: ....

....

....

Guest name(s) ....

Arrived .... Departed ....

Where did you travel from? ....

Best Places to Eat/Drink : ....

....

Places to Visit/Attractions : ....

....

Favorite Memories: ....

....

....

Message to Host: ....

....

....

Guest name(s) ....

Arrived .... Departed ....

Where did you travel from? ....

Best Places to Eat/Drink : ....

....

Places to Visit/Attractions : ....

....

Favorite Memories: ....

....

....

Message to Host: ....

....

....

Guest name(s) ....

Arrived .... Departed ....

Where did you travel from? ....

Best Places to Eat/Drink: ....

....

Places to Visit/Attractions: ....

....

Favorite Memories: ....

....

....

Message to Host: ....

....

....

Guest name(s) ....

Arrived .... Departed ....

Where did you travel from? ....

Best Places to Eat/Drink : ....

....

Places to Visit/Attractions : ....

....

Favorite Memories: ....

....

....

Message to Host: ....

....

....

Guest name(s) ....

Arrived .... Departed ....

Where did you travel from ? ....

Best Places to Eat/Drink : ....

....

Places to Visit/Attractions : ....

....

Favorite Memories: ....

....

....

Message to Host: ....

....

....

Guest name(s) ....

Arrived .... Departed ....

Where did you travel from? ....

Best Places to Eat/Drink: ....

....

Places to Visit/Attractions: ....

....

Favorite Memories: ....

....

....

Message to Host: ....

....

....

Guest name(s) ....

Arrived .... Departed ....

Where did you travel from ? ....

Best Places to Eat / Drink : ....

....

Places to Visit / Attractions : ....

....

Favorite Memories: ....

....

....

Message to Host: ....

....

....